Irish Wrecks *of* the Spanish Armada

Laurence Flanagan

Country House, Dublin

Published in 1995 by
Town House and Country House
Trinity House
Charleston Road
Ranelagh, Dublin 6
Ireland

Text copyright © Laurence Flanagan, 1995

All rights reserved. No part of this publication may be reproduced, stored in a retrieval system,
or transmitted in any form or by any means, electronic, mechanical, photocopying, recording or
otherwise without prior permission in writing from the publishers.

British Library Cataloguing in Publication Data. A catalogue record for this book is available
from the British Library.

ISBN: 0-946172-47-1

00122567

941.505 / 953329

Illustration acknowledgements
The author and publishers would like to thank the following for permission to reproduce their
photographs: Marc Jasinski, plates 1, 2, 3, 4, 5, 6, 10, 11, figs 7, 8; The Ulster Museum, plates
7 (cover), 8; Colin Martin, plates 12, 13, 14, 15, 16, 17, 18, figs 10, 11, 12, 13; The Royal Irish
Academy, fig 2; Robert Sténuit, fig 5.

Cover: *a selection of artefacts mainly recovered from the wreck of the* Girona. Inset: *a galleass
from the John Pine engravings of the Spanish Armada.*

Series editor: Dr Michael Ryan
Text editor: Elaine Campion
Design & artwork: Bill and Tina Murphy
Colour origination: The Kulor Centre
Printed in Ireland by ßetaprint

LEABHARLANNA CHONTAE PHORTLÁIRGE

3 0004 00095 3329

IRISH WRECKS OF THE SPANISH ARMADA

8888

For Marc Jasinski, Colin Martin, Robert Sténuit and Sydney Wignall
whose enterprise and skill have done so much to advance Armada studies in Ireland, and for
Des Brannigan, the City of Derry Sub-Aqua Club and the Portrush Sub-Aqua Club.

CONTENTS

PROLOGUE

The dispatch of the great Spanish fleet, or Armada, in 1588 by Philip II of Spain, with the intention of invading England, was quite an incredible achievement. The fleet that crossed the bar at Lisbon in May of that year consisted of 130 ships, sixty-five of which were either warships or large merchant ships converted for use as warships, twenty-five transports, four galleys and four galleasses, as well as thirty-two smaller vessels, mainly fast dispatch ships. The fleet was arranged in ten squadrons, grouped either according to their source, eg the Squadron of Portugal, or type, eg the Squadron of Urcas (transports). Aboard the ships were 19,295 soldiers and their officers, as well as some 8050 sailors. The fleet was armed with 2431 pieces of weaponry, of both bronze and iron, of various sizes and calibres. It also carried enormous quantities of shot, powder and other weapons, as well as food, and all the additional trappings of war — each meticulously listed by Spanish civil servants. The commander-in-chief of this mighty enterprise was the Duke of Medina Sidonia, a most illustrious nobleman who had been awarded the Order of the Golden Fleece, the highest Spanish honour, normally restricted to reigning monarchs and princes of the royal blood. The duke, however, was a most reluctant commander, pleading every excuse to avoid the colossal responsibility, which included a rather hazardous rendezvous with another invasion force commanded by the Duke of Parma, which was to be conveyed in barges from the low countries. Eventually he recognised that there was no alternative to assuming the command and he travelled to Lisbon to complete the preparations.

As soon as the great fleet left Lisbon harbour they encountered their first setback — a strengthening wind from the north-north-west which, reaching gale force, actually blew the entire fleet south; fortunately it eventually shifted to south-south-west and they were able to sail in the intended direction. A fierce storm, however, separated part of the fleet off La Coruna and disabled many of the ships (including the *Santa Maria de la Rosa* and the *Girona*). Medina Sidonia wrote a very despairing letter to the king, but Philip was adamant: the enterprise was to continue, and with as little delay as possible.

On July 29th the Lizard, the most southerly point of mainland England, was sighted, and the following day the Spanish fleet and the hastily assembled English fleet caught sight of each other. Against the 130 ships of the Spanish fleet were ranged some 175 English vessels, which included the largest ship in either fleet, the *Triumph*, commanded by Sir Martin Frobisher, as well as an additional twenty-two victuallers, all within easy reach of home ports. The English, sensibly, decided to avoid direct confrontation (which was precisely what the Spanish, in their famous crescent formation, wanted). Instead they divided into two columns, one under the Lord Admiral, Howard of Effingham, the other under Sir Francis Drake, their intention being to shadow the Armada and pick off any stragglers.

Before long, the Armada lost two ships, by accident rather than by English action. *Nuestra Senora de la Rosario* was rammed by another ship and the *San Salvador* blew up, though it is not totally clear whether this was the result of an accident (all too likely in a wooden ship laden with explosives and flammable materials) or of deliberate sabotage. Both were towed to port by the English while the rest of the Armada sailed on, leaving them to their fates. At this point both sides changed their tactics: Medina Sidonia decided to land on the Isle of Wight and use it as a beach-head; the English split their fleet into four squadrons. There ensued an action by the squadron of Naples, composed of the four galleasses in the Armada. The galleasses had their moment of glory when, supported by the *San Juan*, all four of them attacked the *Triumph*; for a brief period the *Triumph* was at risk, but it escaped. Many of the Spanish commanders blamed Medina Sidonia for not seizing his opportunity. In the course of this action the Armada had sailed past its access to the Isle of Wight and the commander-in-chief decided to anchor off Calais, against the advice of many of the squadron commanders, and there to meet up with Parma's army.

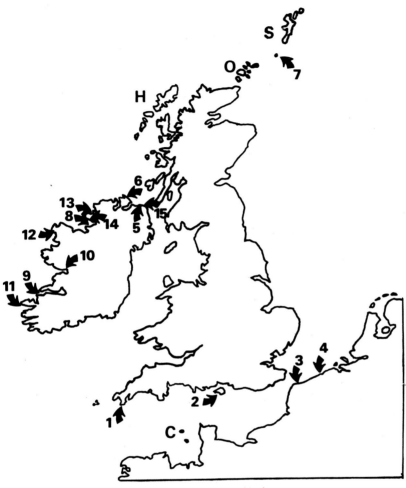

Fig 1   *Map showing the locations of places mentioned in the text.*

1. *The Lizard*
2. *The Isle of Wight*
3. *Calais*
4. *Flanders*
5. *Dunluce, Co Antrim*
6. *Kinnagoe Bay, Co Donegal*
7. *Fair Isle*
8. *Streedagh, Co Sligo*
9. *The Shannon Estuary*
10. *Galway, Co Galway*
11. *Blasket Sound, Co Kerry*
12. *Blacksod Bay, Co Mayo*

13. *Loughros More, Co Donegal*
14. *Killybegs, Co Donegal*
15. *Lacada Point, Co Antrim*

Also indicated are:
C. *The Channel Islands*
H. *The Outer Hebrides*
O. *The Orkneys*
S. *The Shetlands (north of which the fleet was to sail)*

9

The advice of the squadron commanders had been well founded; the next night while the Armada lay at anchor, the English sent eight blazing fireships into its midst. Panic and confusion abounded; cables were cut and anchors abandoned. In the confusion, the *San Lorenzo*, the *capitana* of the squadron of galleasses, fouled its rudder; its commander, Hugo de Moncada, arranged to shelter under the protection of the guns of Calais castle while attempts were made to repair it. De Moncada was unaware of the presence of the fireships, and without a local pilot his ship grounded on a shoal and keeled over. The English boarded her and, despite fierce resistance in which de Moncada himself was killed, looted her, until the castle guns were turned on her and the ship and her ordnance were left to the governor and garrison of Calais. In the confusion occasioned by the fireships, a group of eleven other Spanish ships were suffering the undivided attention of more than a hundred English ships off Gravelines, but despite the countless broadsides fired by the English, they had failed to sink or capture a single Spanish ship by the time the rest of the Armada sailed in to their rescue. By nightfall, however, the *Maria Juan* sank, while the *San Mateo* and *San Felipe*, dangerously low in the water, drifted onto the sandbanks of Flanders. The rest of the fleet came perilously near to sharing the same fate from a strengthening wind blowing from the north-west. Just as total disaster seemed inevitable, the wind shifted to west-south-west, and with many a sigh of relief the Spanish weighed whatever anchors remained and moved into the clear waters of the North Sea. The time for the big decision had arrived: were they to regroup, turn around, sail back into the channel, again attempt to rendezvous with Parma and proceed with the invasion? The decision was made overnight: sailing instructions were issued to take the survivors home to Spain. The Enterprise of England had failed.

10

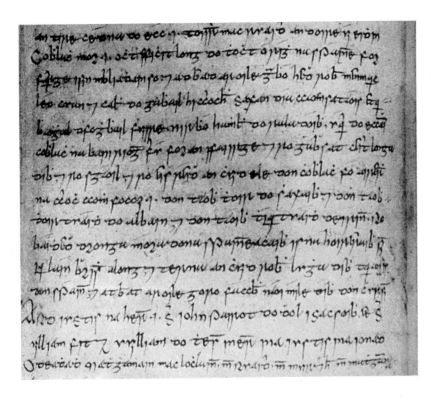

Fig 2 *A succinct
description of the
Armada in Ireland, in
a mere fifteen lines,
from the Annals of
the Four Masters.*

THE VOYAGE HOMEWARD

The sailing instructions issued by the Duke of Medina Sidonia were quite
explicit about one thing: that the fleet should avoid the coasts of Ireland 'for fear
of the harm that might befall you'. Carrying out such instructions in the weather
conditions that prevailed in the autumn of 1588 was not quite as simple. The
journey homeward was a story of disaster piled upon disaster. The first blow
was when the daily rations were reduced; to save water, the horses and mules
had to be thrown overboard. The second blow was that the further north they
sailed, the colder it got; they ran into not only fog, but freezing fog. On
September 3rd the duke reported to the king that since August 21st they had
suffered four nights of storms and seventeen ships had disappeared.

11

Fig 3 *Map showing the locations of the better identified Armada wrecks around the coast of Ireland.*

1. Girona
2. Castillo Negro
3. Barca de Amburg?
4. La Trinidad Valencera
5. Duquesa Santa Ana
6. Santa Maria de Vision
7. La Lavia
8. Juliana
9. La Rata Encoronada
10. El Gran Grin
11. Falco Blanco Mediano
12. San Esteban?
13. Santa Maria de la Rosa
14. San Juan

Three of these were urcas — the transports that carried much of the invasion equipment. The three in question were the *Barca de Amburg*, the *Gran Grifon* and the *Castillo Negro*. With them was a large Venetian merchant ship, the *Trinidad Valencera*. By September 1st the *Barca* was taking in water quicker then her pumps could handle and she could no longer be kept afloat; her company was transferred to the *Gran Grifon* and the *Trinidad Valencera*. Almost immediately she went down, somewhere off the north coast of Ireland. A few days later the other three were separated. The *Castillo Negro* disappeared, although she may be the 'one shippe wrecked near to Dunluce wherein about 300 men perished' (her complement was 310). The fate of the other two is more accurately recorded: the *Trinidad Valencera* was caught in a bad storm on the night of September 12th and was so damaged that she had to run for land. She found it at Kinnagoe Bay on the eastern tip of Malin Head, where she grounded on a reef. The *Gran Grifon* was caught in a severe storm on September 7th and was driven backwards and forwards for several days until it ran aground on Fair Isle.

Many other Armada ships fared little better. A violent storm on September 20th drove three great ships, the *Juliana*, the *Lavia* and the *Santa Maria de Vision*, onto the shelving strand at Streedagh, County Sligo, pounding and tearing them to pieces. In this monstrous wreck nearly one thousand perished, but one notable survivor was Captain Francisco Cuellar, who eventually reached Flanders and wrote an account of his adventures. Similar disasters were taking place all along the west coast of Ireland. Seven ships sought refuge and water in the estuary of the Shannon, but were refused permission to send landing parties ashore and were forced to put to sea again despite the raging storm. In Galway the entire crew of the *Falco Blanco Mediano* were summarily executed, in accordance with the directive issued from Dublin Castle by the Lord Deputy 'to apprehend and execute all Spaniards found there, of what quality soever'. Only her captain was spared, presumably on the grounds that he might be worth a ransom.

Further down the west coast, in Blasket Sound, County Kerry, a rather *13* bizarre drama was unfolding. The first Spanish ship to enter the small anchorage was the *San Juan de Portugal*, commanded by Juan Martinez de Recalde; this was followed soon after by *San Juan Bautista*. Then, on September 21st, a third ship appeared, the *Santa Maria de la Rosa*, clearly in great distress, her sails in tatters except for her foresail. As she came in, one shot was fired from her, then another; she cast her sole remaining anchor and seemed to be riding peacefully until, at two o'clock, without further warning, she sank with all on board, 'a most extraordinary and terrifying thing'. Shortly afterwards, another *San Juan Bautista* (the third *San Juan* in one small haven) came in, in such bad shape that it was decided to evacuate her crew and scuttle her.

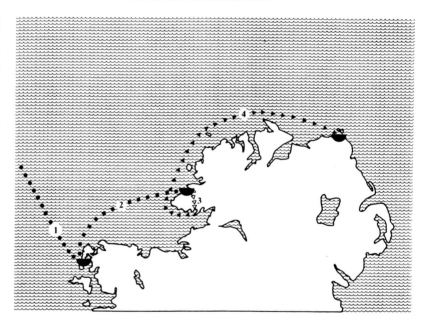

Fig 4 Map showing the sites of the three wrecks suffered by Don Alonso de Leiva and the route of his overland journey to Killybegs.

1. Route of Sancta Maria Encoronada *to her wreck in Blacksod Bay*

2. Route of Duquesa Santa Ana *to her wreck at Loughros More*

3. Alonso de Leiva's overland route from Kiltoorish Lake to Killybegs

4. Route of Girona *from Killybegs to her wreck on Lacada Point*

Up in County Mayo, a tripartite tragedy had commenced on September 17th when the *Rata Encoronada* entered Blacksod Bay and ran aground. She was commanded by Don Alonso de Leiva (the provisional commander-in-chief of the Armada in the event of Medina Sidonia's demise), who immediately showed his leadership qualities by safely disembarking his crew, systematically

14

stripping the ship of anything of value, and then firing it so that no useful spoils might accrue to the enemy. He then occupied a small castle at Doona, until he heard that another Armada ship, the *Duquesa Santa Ana*, was nearby. He re-embarked his men on her and set sail again; whether by accident or design they sailed north, only to suffer a second wreck at Loughros More in County Donegal. Again he successfully disembarked his men and found yet another abandoned fortification to occupy, this time on an island in Kiltoorish Lake, where an iron gun-type known as a falcon, salvaged from the ship to help defend his temporary stronghold, survived until about 1970, when it was stolen.

Fig 5 *The iron gun-type known as the falcon, salvaged by Don Alonso de Leiva and taken by him for the defence of his camp in Kiltoorish Lake.*

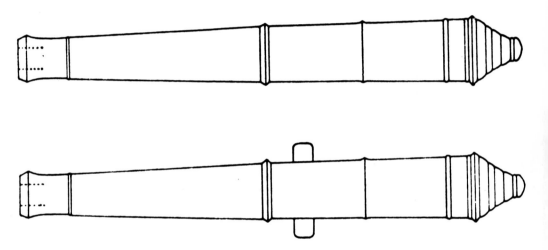

While he was encamped at Kiltoorish he heard that another Armada ship, the galleass *Girona*, was in Killybegs, some twenty miles away across mountain bogland. He went there, organised necessary repairs to the *Girona*, and set sail once again. This time he deliberately sailed north, intending to make for south-west Scotland, which at the time was an independent kingdom quite well-disposed to Spain, from where he hoped to get himself and his men safely to mainland Europe. As they crept along the northern coast of Ireland, the 'cruel talon of rock' that is Lacada Point, County Antrim, proved their final stopping place on October 26th. Here the *Girona* went down with the loss of some 1300

15

men, the greatest and last tragic wreck of the Spanish Armada on the Irish coast. While many Armada ships did successfully return to Spain, about twenty perished on or near the Irish coast, with a loss of some 11,000 lives.

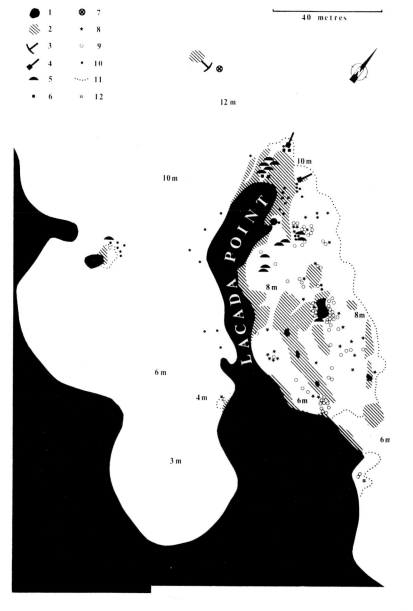

Fig 6   *The wreck-site of the galleass* Girona. *The black represents dry land, the hatched areas are sloping bedrock or outcrops of bedrock, and the dotted line indicates the limit of the excavation. The other symbols indicate find-spots of artefacts, including ordnance, an anchor and lead ingots.*

16

cont. p 31

Pl 1 *The wreck-site of the* Girona: *the Chimney Rock is in the foreground while the expedition's boat is to the right of Lacada Point, Co Antrim.*

Pl 2 *A diver surfaces, happily brandishing one of the heavy gold chains recovered from the* Girona.

17

18

Pl 4   *One surviving member of the necklace of lapis lazuli portrait-cameos in gold mounts recovered from the* Girona.

Pl 5   The heavy gold ring inscribed 'Madame de Champagney MDXXIIII' (1524) which had been worn by her grandson, Don Tomas Perrenoto, when he perished in the wreck of the Girona; this ring constituted the positive proof that the vessel was the Girona.

Pl 6   A silver lid bearing an 'A', which probably stands for 'Aqua' (Water), likely to have been part of a set of altar vessels, recovered from the Girona.

(Facing page)
Pl 7   Displayed on a background of silver coins from the Girona are some pieces of sixteenth-century jewellery, among them the ruby-embellished gold salamander found on the Girona site.

(Facing page)
Pl 8 *Gunner's equipment recovered from* La Trinidad Valencera, *including, from the rear, a copper bucket, a wooden sponge-head (used, wrapped in hairy skin soaked in vinegar or urine, to clean out the gun-barrels after firing and to extinguish any remaining sparks before reloading), a powder scoop (made of copper to prevent unwelcome sparks), a wooden linstock (for holding the match to the touch-hole), several rounds of stone and iron shot and three shot-gauges for checking the calibre of the shot.*

Pl 9 *The gold cross of a Knight of Santiago recovered from the* Girona, *which almost certainly belonged to Don Alonso de Leiva.*

23

Pl 10   *Gold cross of a Knight of the Order of St John of Jerusalem which belonged to the Girona's captain.*

24   Pl 11   *Raising an Esmeril from the sea-bottom by means of buoyancy bags.*

Pl 12 *The wreck-site of the* Santa Maria *observed from Coumeenoole, Co Kerry.*

Pl 13 *The pewter plate inscribed 'Matute' — after Francisco Ruiz Matute, who had been a captain of infantry aboard the* Santa Maria *— which proved that the wreck was that of the* Santa Maria.

Pl 14 *Kinnagoe Bay, Co Donegal, where the City of Derry Sub-Aqua Club discovered the resting-place of* La Trinidad Valencera *in 1971.*

27

Pl 15 *The Royal Arms of Philip II of Spain on one of the massive siege-guns recovered from* La Trinidad Valencera. *These guns proved beyond dispute that the wreck was that of the* Trinidad.

(Facing page top) Pl 16 *Remains of the hull of* La Trinidad Valencera *on the sea-bed.*

(Facing page bottom) Pl 17 *A group of finds including a copper bucket and a pewter plate on the sea-bed.*

28

Pl 18   *One of the
massive gun-carriage
wheels being
prepared for lifting
from the sea-bed.*

30

THE IRISH ARMADA WRECKS

The *Girona*

While the general location of several of the wreck-sites of Armada ships in Ireland was known, the first to be accurately located was the *Girona*, a galleass of the Naples squadron. A galleass was a vessel based on the Mediterranean oared galley, propelled by oars as well as sails on three masts, the idea being that if the wind failed, the oars could be used. Thanks to the testimony of an English sailor who had been aboard the *San Lorenzo*, the galleass that grounded at Calais, we know that this vessel was about sixty paces long, with 'oars, sales and ship red'. We know additionally from the inventory of the Armada that the *Girona* originally carried 120 sailors, 169 soldiers and 300 oarsmen. Her resting place was discovered by Robert Sténuit, the celebrated Belgian nautical archaeologist. While early documentary references to the location of her wreck-site are confusing and contradictory, the appearance on the Ordnance Survey maps of County Antrim of a Spaniard Rock, a Spaniard Cave and a Port na Spaniagh, afforded a tempting clue to Sténuit. In June 1967 he visited Port na Spaniagh and made his first dive. The first thing he discovered was a lead ingot, of known Armada type. Then, as he swam along the east face of Lacada Point, he found the barrel of a bronze gun, then another, complete with breech-blocks, as well as a copper coin. He knew he had found the *Girona*.

The following year, 1968, Sténuit returned to Port na Spaniagh accompanied by a full diving team, which included Marc Jasinski, an expert photographer both above and below water, and all the equipment required for the excavation. The excavation extended into 1969 and involved some 6000 hours of diving, in an underwater world that is anything but static: 40-tonne boulders could be shifted by winter storms from one area to another with the greatest of ease, making excavating under such a boulder perilous in the extreme. The one consolation was that the water was reasonably shallow, allowing quite prolonged periods of diving.

31

The results of the excavation of the *Girona* were quite spectacular. While nothing survived of the vessel itself, because of the shallowness of the water and the exposed nature of the site, a treasury of Renaissance jewellery was recovered, including badges of Orders of Chivalry — for example, a gold 'Maltese' cross of the Order of St John of Jerusalem, that probably belonged to the captain, Fabricio Spinola, and a small oval receptacle pertaining to the Spanish Order of Alcantara, one side of which consists of a fretted cross, the other (the lid) of a piece of gold engraved with the figure of a saint and a pear-tree, St Julian del Pereiro, whose owner has not been identified. Perhaps the most impressive piece was a small gold pendant in the form of a salamander, originally embellished with nine rubies, only three of which have survived, and with its paws, wings, mouth, teeth, nose and even its scales clearly modelled. Also found was a series of gold chains, some large and heavy — which rich Spanish gentlemen were wont to wear around their necks and which may in some cases have accelerated the speed with which the gentlemen in question sank to the seabed — others finer and lighter. Another spectacular item was a necklace consisting (originally) of twelve lapis lazuli portrait-cameos of Roman

32

emperors, set in gold frames, of which ten survive more or less intact, together w.th the gold frame of the eleventh. There was a rich collection of gold rings, including one that proves the wreck was that of the *Girona*; this large ring, with a rectangular bezel and setting for a gemstone, no longer present, is inscribed 'Madame de Champagney MDXXIIII', and clearly was being worn by her grandson, Don Tomas Perrenoto, who is specifically recorded as having perished on the *Girona*. Another ring recovered was a very poignant reminder of the personal loss suffered by many people in Spain; this is a simple gold ring with one terminal in the form of a hand holding a heart, the other the shape of a buckle, inscribed 'No tengo mas que dar te' (I have nothing more to give you), and was presumably a present from a Spanish lady to her departing lover.

The array of coins found constitute a very important hoard; of the 1320 recovered, 414 were of gold, 789 of silver and 122 of base metal. They were struck at fourteen different mints, including Seville, Toledo, Madrid and Granada on the Spanish mainland, Naples in Italy and, in the New World, at Mexico, Lima and Potosi, reflecting the fact that these coins were not from an official treasure chest but were the property of people on board. Inevitably those of gold were the best preserved, while those of base metal were the worst.

Of the fifty guns the *Girona* originally carried, only two were recovered: a bronze half-saker, rather badly corroded but with the Arms of Spain and the Chain of the Order of the Golden Fleece just visible on the chase, and a bronze Esmeril, a breech-loading anti-personnel weapon, complete with breech-blocks. Navigation equipment was represented by two bronze astrolabes, one worn but intact, the other in fragments; these were used to measure the angle between the sun and the horizon, from which the ship's latitude could be calculated. There were also several pairs of navigational dividers. A number of bronze coaks (bearings for wooden pulley-blocks) were recovered, as were some iron shackles for the standing rigging. A silver bosun's pipe, surprisingly similar to modern examples, was also found. In addition to the religious medals found on all Armada wreck-sites, the *Girona* produced several crucifixes, a gold ring

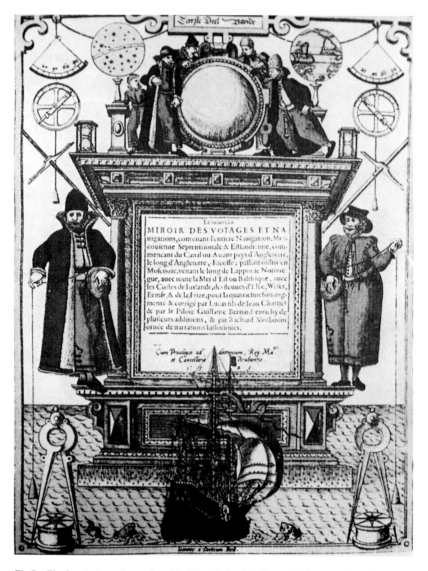

Fig 8 *The frontispiece of a work entitled* The Mariner's Mirror, *which was published in October 1588, just after the end of the Armada campaign. It displays all the navigational equipment available to sixteenth-century mariners. On both sides at the top are astrolabes, of which two were recovered from the* Girona; *the two gentlemen at the sides are using sounding-leads (for discovering the depth of water and, if necessary, the nature of the seabed). On either side at the bottom are magnetic compasses, one example of which was recovered from* La Trinidad Valencera. *Each compass is framed by a pair of navigational dividers, for marking off distances on charts, examples of which were recovered from both the* Girona *and the* Trinidad.

inscribed 'IHS', which may have belonged to a Jesuit on board, an Agnus Dei gold reliquary and a silver lid surmounted by the letter 'A', which almost certainly stands for 'Aqua' (Water), suggesting it is the lid of an altar-cruet and implying that there was likely to have been a complete set of altar-vessels for the service of Mass on board the ship. Though small in quantity, this group of artefacts reflects the strong religious element in the intent and practice of the Armada, as confirmed by Medina Sidonia when he instructed the fleet that 'The principal aim of His Majesty is the service of God'.

While the presence of significant amounts of jewellery on a fighting ship may be surprising, even more surprising is the evidence of the rather grand lifestyle of the officers and gentlemen on board: there are fragments of splendid dishes, both of silver and of silver-gilt, as well as silver candlesticks and tapersticks. Even more remarkable was the number of silver table forks recovered, all in fragments, but including forks with two, three, four and even five prongs. Subsequent to the completion of Sténuit's excavation, a nearly intact two-pronged fork was recovered, and even more recently a totally intact

Fig 9 *An intact silver three-pronged fork recovered from the* Girona.

35

three-pronged one, in more or less pristine condition, which must be the oldest intact silver table fork in the world. Another important post-Sténuit discovery was of a gold Cross of a Knight of Santiago, which almost certainly belonged to Don Alonso de Leiva and had survived all three of his shipwrecks.

The *Santa Maria de la Rosa*

While Port na Spaniagh can be wild and tempestuous in winter gales, the water is at least shallow and the wreck close to the shore. Blasket Sound, on the other hand, is seldom placid, the water is deep, and it was not known precisely where

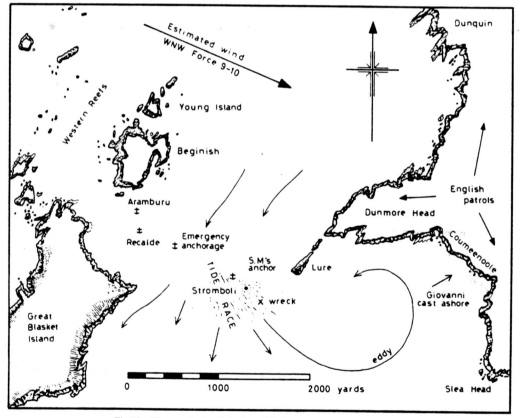

Fig 10   *The wreck-site of the* Santa Maria de la Rosa *in Blasket Sound.*

in the four square miles of Blasket Sound the *Santa Maria* had so spectacularly sunk. Efforts to locate the site began in 1963, but despite intensive searching in often hair-raisingly dangerous conditions, it was not until 1968, when four different anchors were located and finally a mound of ballast containing iron shot, lead musket balls and several lead ingots of the classic Armada boat-shape, that there was reasonable hope that an Armada wreck had been found. There was a slight doubt that the wreck might be that of the *San Juan* rather than of the *Santa Maria de la Rosa* — which was the desired objective, since being an almiranta, a vice-flagship, the *San Juan* was likely to have been carrying official treasure and, being in water at least 30m deep, there was a strong chance that some, at least, of the hull might be preserved. Confirmation that the wreck was indeed that of the *Santa Maria* was soon forthcoming. Two pewter plates inscribed with the name 'Matute' were found. From documentary sources it was known that one Francisco Ruiz Matute had been a captain of infantry aboard the *Santa Maria de la Rosa*, in charge of a company of ninety-five men. In addition, they found several arquebuses and a larger bored musket, and, rather gruesomely, under another larger plate, the legs, pelvis and ribs of an unfortunate sailor who, they conjectured, must have been crushed to death by ballast when the ship sank so suddenly. Under the ballast mound they found the mast-step as well as confirmation that after the storm at La Coruna the *Santa Maria* had a replacement main mast fitted. Unfortunately, little of the material recovered from the *Santa Maria* has survived, which serves to emphasise the need to have adequate conservation facilities organised before any large-scale wreck excavation takes place.

La Trinidad Valencera

While the precise resting-place of the *Santa Maria* took years of hard and dangerous work to locate, the City of Derry Sub-Aqua Club more or less stumbled on the site of *La Trinidad Valencera*. In the course of a training dive

Fig 11 *One of the large siege-guns recovered from* La Trinidad Valencera.

PHILIPPVS
·REX·

IOANES·MARICVS·A·LARA·FIERI·CVRAVIT
OPVS·REMIGY·DE·HALVT
ANNO 1 5 5 6

38

in February 1971, one of the members of the club spotted, by accident, a piece of bronze ordnance resting on top of a rock. In the flurry of excitement that understandably ensued, other guns were discovered. One of these was adorned with the royal arms of Philip II of Spain, the inscription 'Philippus Rex' and the date '1556', giving good reason to be confident that they had found the wreck of the *Trinidad*. The club decided that a properly conducted scientific excavation was the only acceptable course of action.

The finds from the several seasons of excavation were most rewarding. Part of the ship's planking survived, showing that unlike the *Santa Maria de la Rosa*, the *Trinidad*'s fastening was by means of metal rivets rather than wooden dowels. Many items from the rigging were recovered — single and double blocks, hearts and even lengths of cable. Other pieces of ship's equipment included tools such as hammers and mallets, a pair of bellows, copper buckets, lanterns and even a straw whisk. The most spectacular items, however, were the ordnance, particularly the two great siege-guns, cast in Mechelen in 1556 by Remigy de Halut and belonging to the royal siege-train of Philip II. There were also two Venetian guns (the *Trinidad* was a Venetian merchantship) by noted Venetian founders, Zuanne Alberghetti and Nicole di Conti, and a bronze swivel-gun with its iron support and part of its tiller intact. The excavations also uncovered an impressive collection of other items associated with gunnery: copper powder-scoops, wooden shot-gauges and linstocks, a wooden gunner's rule, sponge-heads for cleaning the gun-barrels, and even pieces of hairy goatskin for wrapping round them. There were several gun-carriage wheels as well as countless rounds of shot, and even an example of canister-shot, filled with shrapnel. Navigation equipment recovered included the base of a mariner's compass and a remarkably fine pair of dividers, still in working condition.

Many of the items of invasion equipment listed in the detailed inventory preserved in the Spanish archives were recovered, including several parts of muskets and arquebuses, powder flasks, a ceramic hand grenade and even a tent complete with tent-pegs. Food containers included pottery jars (one actually *39*

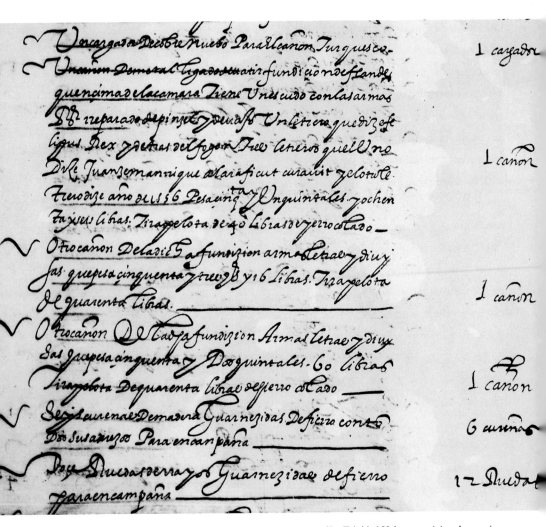

Fig 12   *An extract from the detailed inventory of* La Trinidad Valencera *giving the precise descriptions of the siege-guns, by means of which the identity of the wreck was confirmed.*

40

contained lentils) and the staves and bases of barrels. Steelyards for weighing out goods were recovered, as were pestles and mortars for grinding. There was a varied collection of pewter, including flagons, beakers, goblets and a spoon, as well as wooden dishes, bowls and plates. Some of the pewter was actually made in England, with marks of Edward Roe, a Master of the London Company of Pewterers. There were ceramic drug-jars and the remains of musical instruments — a tambourine and the neck of some kind of stringed instrument. Preserved intact, by some bizarre accident, was a Chinese porcelain bowl, undoubtedly the property of a rich person who had enjoyed contacts with China, possibly through Portuguese merchants.

The most surprising discovery, in many ways, was the wealth of textiles recovered, including cords, tassels, braids and ribbons of silk, as well as several woollen fragments such as a pocket-flap and a sock. There was even a part of a woollen pennant, with an eagle-like emblem. All in all, the finds from the *Trinidad* were a perfect complement to those from the *Girona*; together they constitute a fairly well-rounded picture of life on sixteenth-century Spanish warships.

The *Juliana*, the *Lavia* and the *Santa Maria de Vision*

Although it had long been known that three great Armada ships had been wrecked on Streedagh Strand in County Sligo, it was not until 1985 that they were precisely located by the Streedagh Armada Group using sophisticated detecting equipment. The three ships in question were the *Juliana*, the *Lavia* and the *Santa Maria de Vision*. Three bronze guns were lifted from the site; these comprised two pedreros, specially designed to fire the stone shot that is such a feature of Armada wreck-sites, and a handsome saker dated to 1570. The rudder of the *Juliana*, intact, with iron pintles still in position, was observed but not moved; the fact that it is 12m long gives a rather awesome indication of the scale of the problems to be encountered in the course of a nautical excavation. *41*

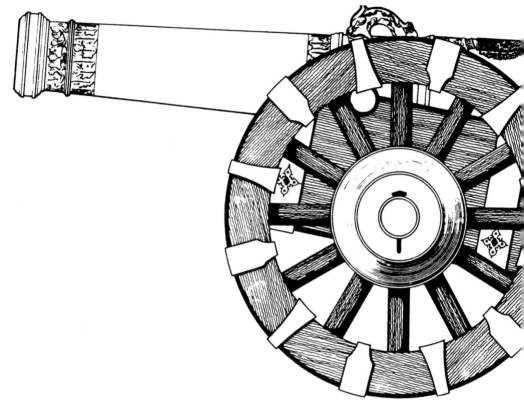

Fig 13   *Reconstruction drawing of one of the siege-guns recovered from* La Trinidad Valencera, *mounted on a carriage.*

Without adequate pre-arranged conservation facilities it is the utmost folly even to contemplate the excavation of such a site. None were available, and partly at least for this reason, the Streedagh site was protected by the Irish government and all work on it suspended. It has been, and still is, the subject of prolonged legal argument, in and out of the Irish High Court. There is little doubt that the Streedagh site is of profound archaeological importance, even if, as seems likely, the costs of conservation would far exceed the commercial value of the potential finds. It is likely that other Irish Armada sites will also be preserved, *in situ*, until the necessary conservation facilities are available. Ireland's Armada

42

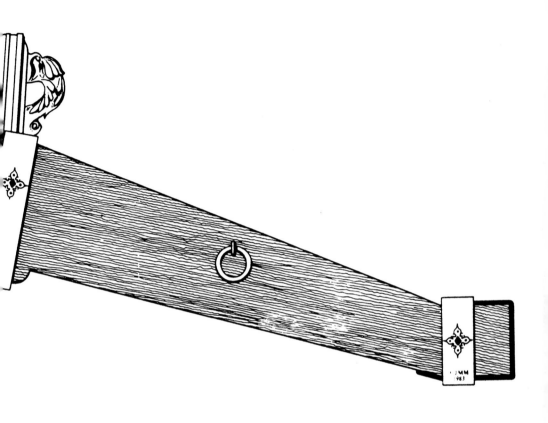

heritage is rich, and of importance not merely to Ireland but to the world, constituting as it does a resource that must be developed with care and responsibility.

Arquebus: A long gun in use in the sixteenth century, which was lighter than the musket, both in terms of the weight of the weapon and of the shot fired by it (c15g); it was light enough to be fired from the shoulder without support. Those is use in the Armada would have been 'match-locks', ie fired by the application of a light to the charge.

Astrolabe: A heavy circular metal ring with calibrations on its rim and a metal pointer used to measure the angular height of the sun above the horizon at noon, when the sun is at its highest. Based on this observation, the ship's latitude could be calculated from astronomical tables.

Breech-loading: Most of the heavy guns in use in the sixteenth century were muzzle-loading; both the charge of powder and the round of shot were loaded into the gun-barrel at the end from which they were subsequently to emerge. Some guns, however, mainly smaller pieces, had their charge of powder loaded at the breech end, for which purpose a detachable powder chamber, or breech-block, was used. This type of loading made possible a faster rate of fire.

Coak: A heavy square piece of bronze or brass with a central, circular perforation, used as a bearing for wooden rigging blocks to prevent the wood splitting.

Esmeril: A type of small-calibre gun (c52mm) mounted on a swivel to facilitate traversing. To allow for rapid reloading, it was breech-loading, with a separate powder chamber. It served mainly as an anti-personnel weapon.

Falcon: One of several gun-types named after birds, this was one of the lighter pieces of ordnance, firing iron shot of about 1.3kg in weight.

Galleass: A type of ship that combined the oar-propulsion of the Mediterranean galley with the sail propulsion of the galleon. Those used in the Armada were square-rigged on the fore and main masts and lateen-rigged on the mizzen mast (ie the sail carried on the mast at the stern was triangular). They carried 300 rowers to ply the eighteen or so oars on each side.

Heart: A heavy heart-shaped piece of wood with a groove around the circumference, around which one rope would be secured, and with a hole in the middle through which another rope would pass. Used, for example, to secure stays.

Musket: The heavier type of long gun, which fired a shot about four times the weight of that fired by an arquebus (*c*60g). The weapon itself was so heavy that it required a Y-shaped support for the barrel.

Pedreros: Guns, of various calibres, used, as the name suggests, to fire the stone shot so abundant on Armada wreck-sites.

Pintle: A pin attached to the leading edge of the rudder, slotting into metal rings on the stern of the ship, allowing the rudder to be turned by means of the tiller.

Saker: Another gun-type named after a bird, but in this case the lanner, or sacred, falcon. Smaller or 'half' versions also existed.

Urca: A transport, of which an entire squadron was attached to the Armada for the transport of soldiers and supplies. The term is sometimes, rather unflatteringly, rendered as 'hulk'.

Victuallers: Small ships used to provision, or 'victual', the fleet, particularly in home waters.

INDEX

Page references to illustrations are in *italics*.

Annals of the Four Masters, *11*
artefacts, *16*, *26*, *29*, 33, 35, *35*, 37, 39–41,
   see also coins; jewellery; navigational
   equipment; ordnance; religious artefacts

Barca de Amburg, 12
Blacksod Bay, Co Mayo, *9*, 14, *14*
Blasket Sound, Co Kerry, *9*, 13–14, 36, *36*,
   37

Calais, France, 8, *9*, 10, 31
Castillo Negro, *12*, 13
Champagney, Madame de, 20, 33
Chimney Rock, Co Antrim, *17*
City of Derry Sub-Aqua Club, 27, 37–9
coins, *21*, 31, 33
Coumeenoole, Co Kerry, 26
Cuellar, Francisco (Capt), 13

de Leiva, Don Alonso, 14, *14*, 15, 36
de Moncada, Hugo, 10
de Recalde, Juan Martinez, 14
Doona, Co Mayo, 15
Drake, Sir Francis, 8
Dublin Castle, 13
Dunluce, Co Antrim, *9*, 13
Duquesa Santa Ana, *12*, *14*, 15

Fair Isle, *9*, 13
Falco Blanco Mediano, *12*, 13
Flanders, *9*, 10, 13
Frobisher, Sir Martin, 8

Galway, Co Galway, *9*, 13
Girona, 8, *12*, *14*, 15, 18
   wreck-site, *16*, *17*, 20, 23, 24, 31–6
Gran Grifon, 13
Gran Grin, 12
Gravelines, France, 10
guns, *see* ordnance

Howard of Effingham (Lord Admiral), 8

inventory of fleet, 7, 39, *40*
Isle of Wight, England, 8, *9*

Jasinski, Marc, 31
jewellery, *21*, 35
   badges of Orders of Chivalry, *23*, *24*,
      32, 36
   gold chains, *17*, *18*, 32

   gold rings, *20*, 33
   necklace of lapis lazuli, *19*, 32–3
   salamander pendant, *21*, 32
Juliana, *12*, 13, 41–3

Killybegs, Co Donegal, *9*, 14, *14*, 15
Kiltoorish Lake, Co Donegal, *14*, 15
Kinnagoe Bay, Co Donegal, *9*, 13, *27*

Lacada Point, Co Antrim, *9*, *14*, 15, *17*, 31
La Coruna, Spain, 7, 37
Lavia, *12*, 13, 41–3
Lisbon, Portugal, 7
Lizard, The, England, 8, *9*
Loughros More, Co Donegal, *9*, *14*, 15

Malin Head, Co Donegal, 13
Maria Juan, 10
Mariner's Mirror, The, *34*
Matute, Francisco Ruiz, 26, 37
Medina Sidonia, Duke of, 7, 8, 11, 14, 35

navigational equipment, 33, *34*, 39
Nuestra Senora de la Rosario, 8

ordnance, 31, 33, 37, 38, 39, 41
   Esmeril, *24–5*
   falcon, 15, *15*
   gun-carriage wheels, *30*, 39
   gunner's equipment, *22*, 39
   half-saker, 33
   saker, 41
   siege-guns, *28*, *38*, 39, *42–3*

Parma, Duke of, 7, 8, 10
Perrenoto, Don Tomas, 20, 33
Philip II of Spain, 7, 8, 11, 28, 39
Port na Spaniagh, Co Antrim, 31, 36

Rata Encoronada, *12*, 14, *14*
religious artefacts, *20*, 33–5

Sancta Maria Encoronada, *see Rata*
   Encoronada
San Esteban, *12*
San Felipe, 10
San Juan, 8, *12*, 37
San Juan Bautista, 14
San Juan de Portugal, 14
San Lorenzo, 10, 31
San Mateo, 10
San Salvador, 8
Santa Maria de la Rosa, 8, *12*, 14, 26
   wreck-site, *26*, 36–7, *36*, 39